Henry Benjamin Wheatley, Philip Henry Delamotte

Artwork in Gold and Silver

Henry Benjamin Wheatley, Philip Henry Delamotte

Artwork in Gold and Silver

ISBN/EAN: 9783743313552

Manufactured in Europe, USA, Canada, Australia, Japa

Cover: Foto ©Thomas Meinert / pixelio.de

Manufactured and distributed by brebook publishing software (www.brebook.com)

Henry Benjamin Wheatley, Philip Henry Delamotte

Artwork in Gold and Silver

ART WORK

IN

GOLD AND SILVER

𝕸𝖔𝖉𝖊𝖗𝖓.

BY

HENRY B. WHEATLEY, F.S.A.

ASSISTANT SECRETARY, SOCIETY OF ARTS,

AND

PHILIP H. DELAMOTTE,

PROFESSOR OF DRAWING AND PAINTING, AND LECTURER ON
PRACTICAL FINE ART, KING'S COLLEGE, LONDON.

New York:

CHARLES SCRIBNER'S SONS,

743—745, BROADWAY.

London: SAMPSON LOW, MARSTON, SEARLE, & RIVINGTON.

1882.

LONDON :
PRINTED BY GILBERT AND RIVINGTON, LIMITED,
ST. JOHN'S SQUARE.

EDITORS' NOTE.

———•———

THE chief aim of this series of HANDBOOKS OF PRACTICAL ART is to bring to the notice of students and amateurs of art, as well as all lovers of the highest excellence in workmanship, numerous examples, both ancient and modern, of the application of beautiful design to articles of every-day use and to the various objects which are frequently employed for purposes of decoration.

Each Handbook will contain an historical record of the progress of the art of which it treats, from the earliest times to the present, showing the distinctive characteristics of the respective periods; and will be illustrated with about forty to sixty engravings, which will include representations of many of the most remarkable specimens of industrial art that have been preserved to us, and which now adorn the national museums of Europe.

In making the selection, much care has been taken to include only those works that are noteworthy either for the elegance of their form or the beauty of their ornamentation : although a few objects have been chosen for their historical interest, and for the purpose of showing the style of art prevalent at the time in which they were made.

H. B. W.
P. H. D.

CONTENTS.

CHAPTER V.

CHAPTER VI.

CHAPTER VII.

CHAPTER VIII.

CHAPTER IX.

LIST OF ILLUSTRATIONS.

(*Fig.* 41.) SPANISH NECKLACE, SILVER GILT, FILAGREE.

THE RENAISSANCE OF ART

IN THE SIXTEENTH CENTURY.

WE have already alluded to that wide-spread movement which changed the artistic aspect of Europe ; and we mentioned two or three of the distinguished men who preceded Cellini in carrying out the principles of the art of the Renaissance. We cannot therefore do better than commence the account of modern art with a few words respecting the most famous of the artists of the revival.

Benvenuto Cellini was born at Florence in the year 1500. His father was an engineer and an artist in ivory, as well as one of the court musicians, and wished his son to become a professional flute-player. To this Benvenuto would not consent, and at the age of fifteen he apprenticed himself to Antonio di Sandro, surnamed Marcone, a famous goldsmith of his time. At sixteen he was banished for six months from his native city for fighting in the streets in defence of a younger brother. He visited Siena and Bologna, and then returned to Florence. One of the first works of which Cellini speaks in his memoirs,[1] is a silver clasp, upon which he had represented in low relief cupids and grotesque heads intermingled with foliage. At nineteen he went to Rome, where he devoted himself chiefly to the study of ancient examples of his art during two years, and then returned to Florence. In 1523 another quarrel obliged him to leave his

[1] Memoirs of Benvenuto Cellini, written by himself. Translated by Thomas Roscoe. Bohn's Library. 1847.

F

home, and he took refuge in Rome, where he remained for several years.   There he entered the service of Clement VII., and

designed coins and medals for that pope.[2]   His fame now spread far and wide, and Francis I. was anxious to obtain his services.   In consequence he visited Paris in 1537, but he made no long stay.   Three years afterwards he again visited France, and worked there till 1545, when he finally left that country on account of a quarrel with Madame d'Estampes, the king's mistress.   Cellini then returned to Italy and entered the service of Cosmo de Medici, with whom he remained until his death on February 15, 1570.   Very few of his numerous works have come down to us : one of the most important of those that remain is the golden salt-cellar, made for Francis I., which is now in the Cabinet of Antiquities at Vienna. Besides his "Memoirs," one of the most perfect pieces of autobiography ever penned, he wrote a treatise on his art, in which he describes the method of making jewellery, the engraving of coins, the art of

(*Fig.* 42.) VASE DESIGNED BY BENVENUTO CELLINI.

[2] At the siege of Rome by the Duke of Bourbon, in 1527, Cellini defended the castle of St. Angelo, and, according to his own accounts, shot the duke with an arquebus.

damascening, by which designs in gold or silver are formed on iron, bronze, or other hard metal, and all the processes known in his day.

The highly elaborate jug represented in fig. 42 will give the reader a good idea of one class of Cellini's work. It is over-ornamented and such as might have been expected from the character of the man. He was a blusterer with but little admiration for any work but his own. He had no compunction in melting down the fine productions of his predecessors ; still he was a great artist and his influence was immense. The Pope absolved him from the sin of his many homicides on account of the work he had done in the service of the Church. An illustration of the magnificent sardonyx ewer, known as the " Cellini Ewer," which formed part of the crown jewels of France before the first revolution, and is now in the possession of the Right Hon. A. J. B. Beresford Hope, will be found in the chapter on the enamels.

The residence of Cellini in France from 1540 to 1545 exerted an important influence upon the goldsmiths' art in that country, and this was chiefly shown in jewellery, a branch of the art in which he had no rival. All the designs were executed in the Italian style, and mythological subjects occupied almost exclusively the attention of the artists of this kind of work. We obtain some idea of the articles most in vogue during this age from the inventory made after the death of Francis II. There are pendants, rings, bracelets, and, above all, medallions worn on the hat and in the hair. The belts worn by the ladies were often ornamented to a great extent, and some of the entries in the accounts of Francis I. enable us to judge of the character of these belts, which were invariably made of gold and studded with jewels.

The exquisite jewel shown in the next illustration (Fig. 43) is attributed to Benvenuto Cellini, and if not by him it is certainly a fine example of his school.

Albert Jacquemart in his " History of Furniture " makes a vigorous protest against the opinion that France needed to be taught by Italians, and holds that she has not received sufficient credit for her share in the great revival. He writes :—

" Before following the foreign schools, before Matteo del Nassaro had mounted gems or Benvenuto Cellini had created his vases

and jewels, the French artists, notwithstanding the taste of
Georges d'Amboise for the Italian school, did not want either
for orders or encouragement."

Among the French goldsmiths of the sixteenth century
whose names have come down to us may be mentioned Benedict

(*Fig.* 43.) PENDANT ; ENAMELLED ; ENRICHED WITH JEWELS.
[*Attributed to Cellini.*]

Ramel, who executed a portrait in gold of Francis I. ; Guillaume
Arondelle, goldsmith to Catherine de Médicis ; Gilles Suramond
and Jehan Doublet, from whom Henri II. commanded the plate
for the royal table ; François Desjardins, goldsmith to Charles IX.;
François Guyard, goldsmith to Henri III. ; Delahaie and David

Vimont, goldsmiths to Henri IV.; and François Briot, famous for his skill in embossing pewter and all kinds of plate.[3]

The silver-mounted tankard which was once used by the unfortunate Mary of Scotland bears evidence of the peculiar taste of the period (Fig. 44). It is supposed to be of French origin.

In Germany the goldsmiths were not copyists of the Italian revival, but succeeded in producing a national art of their own. The two cities of Nuremberg and Augsburg were the headquarters of these artificers. The father of Albert Durer, who was a goldsmith at Cula in Hungary, settled in Nuremberg in 1502.

There are two remarkable pieces of German table plate at the South Kensington Museum, which are very distinctly national in their character. The first is a gilt hanap made to represent one of the towers of Nuremberg, in which all the details are most elaborately carried out.

The other is a cup in gilt metal, probably Augsburg work of the end of the fifteenth century. It is particularly rich and imposing, full of elaborate details which were characteristic of the work of the German goldsmith before the influence of the renaissance had become apparent. The annexed engraving (Fig. 45) represents a silver cup of German workmanship, singular in its bulbous ornament, which may be dated about 1500.

(*Fig.* 44.) TANKARD OF HORN WITH SILVER-MOUNTING.
[*Once the property of Mary, Queen of Scots.*]

The little cup or vase in silver gilt (Fig. 46) is dated about thirty years after this. It is enriched with arabesque ornament, and set with a number of cameos in onyx, some of which are

[3] Labarte, " Histoire des Arts," ii. 134.

antique and others apparently of Italian cinque-cento origin.
This also is in the South Kensington Museum.

Etienne Delaune (born 1518) was a Frenchman who settled
at Augsburg and obtained great influence by means of his designs.
All his works, with the exception of one medal of Henri II.,
which is in the Louvre, have perished, but pen and ink sketches
on vellum and prints engraved with his own hand show his
imagination and taste.

Theodor de Bry (born at Liege in 1528, died at Frankfort, 1598,)
was a German goldsmith of the sixteenth century, best known

(*Fig.* 45.) SILVER CUP (MEIGELLIN).
[*German, about* 1500.]

by the richness and delicacy of his designs for chasing, many
of which he carried out himself. A silver table of his workmanship is preserved in the Green Vaults at Dresden. He
was also a bookseller, and the designer of " Nova Alphabeti
Effictio," and other alphabets in which ornament plays an important part.

Some other German goldsmiths of the sixteenth century must
not be forgotten, although we can only register the names of
Virgil Solis of Nuremberg, Hirschvogel of Vienna, Jonas
Silber of Nuremberg, Georg Wechter, Daniel Mignot of Augsburg,
and Paul Vlindt of Nuremberg.

In the latter part of the sixteenth century the Italian influence began to be strongly felt in Germany, and the two following designs for a silver cup (Fig. 47)' and 'jug (Fig. 48), both by Wenzel Jamnitzer, (1508—1585) who was one of a family of goldsmiths of the Nuremberg guild, exhibit this influence in a marked degree.

Spain very early followed the example set by Italy at the period of the Renaissance, and the large amount of silver and gold that poured into the country on the discovery of the New World gave a distinct impetus to the art of the goldsmith, which was chiefly devoted to the enrichment of the churches and cathedrals. Mr. Riaño has discovered the names of a large number of Spanish artists in some manuscripts containing designs presented by them on admission to the Corporation of silversmiths of Catalonia. These names and dates

(*Fig.* 46.) VASE, SILVER-GILT.
[*Augsburg work, about* 1530.]

are as follows :—Joan Masanell, 1534 ; Rafael Ximenis, 1537 ; Antonio de Valder, 1537 ; Benedicte Sabat, 1545 ; Gabriel Comes, 1546 ; Pero Juan Poch, 1551 ; Antonio Conill, 1553 ; Francesco Perez, 1559 ; Juan Ximenez, 1561 ; Francisco Vida, 1561 ; Felipe Ros, 1567, 1597 ; Joan Font, 1572 ; Narciso Valla, 1575 ; Juan Pau, 1586. Mr. Riaño, however, affirms that the greatest goldsmiths of Spain were the members of the d'Arfe family, who originally came from Germany.

When, after years of turmoil, peace was established in England by the accession of Henry VII., and the arts began to be encouraged, it was necessary to invite foreign artists to visit this country.

It was in this king's reign that apostles' spoons first came into general use. Mr. Chaffers mentions one of these spoons, dated 1493, as the earliest known to exist.' At a rather later date

---

' Chaffers' " Hall Marks on Plate," 5th ed. p. 85.

(1516), Amy Brent bequeathed "thirteen silver spoons, with the figure of J'hu and his twelve apostles." There were large quantities of precious metals spread about the country in these times, and the bequest of John, Lord Dyneham, in 1505, of 1590

(*Fig.* 47.) DESIGN FOR A SILVER CUP.
[*By Wenzel Jamnitzer.*]

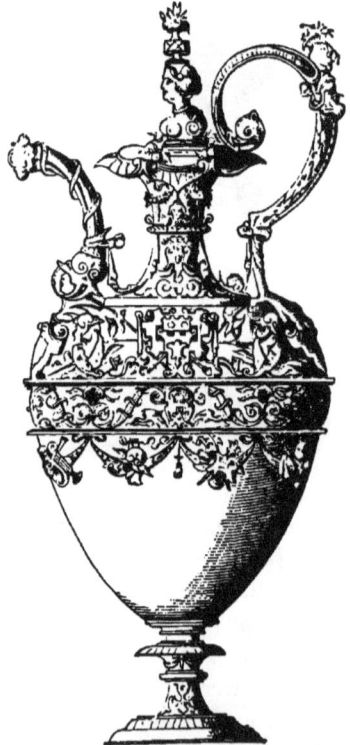

(*Fig.* 48.) DESIGN FOR A SILVER JUG
[*By Wenzel Jamnitzer.*]

ounces of plate to his wife is by no means an isolated instance of these riches.

On the occasion of Prince Arthur's marriage, the feast was served upon gold plate set with precious stones. But it was during the reign of Henry VIII. that some of the most splendid specimens of the goldsmiths' art ever made in England were, produced.

The emulation between Henry and Francis I., which caused them to outvie each other in the luxury of their surroundings, is a matter of history, and it is, therefore, not surprising to find Henry attempting to obtain the services of some of the artists who graced the court of Francis. Holbein, whose portraits of Henry prove the king's passion for personal ornament, made designs for all kinds of goldsmiths' work. One of the most important of these was that for the famous cup presented to Jane Seymour by Henry, which is described as follows :—"A faire standing cupp of goulde, garnished about the cover with eleaven dyamonds, and two poynted diamonds about the cupp, seaventeene table dyamonds, and one pearle pendent uppon the cupp, with theis words, *bound to obey and serve,* and H and I knitt togeather ; in the topp of the cover Queene Jane's armes houlden by twoe boyes under a crowne imperiall ; weighing three score and five ounces and a halfe." [5] The original design, by Holbein, for this cup is in the Bodleian Library, Oxford (Fig. 49). The courtiers were not slow to imitate the splendour of the royal table, and Wolsey, besides some thousands of ounces of plate in use, possessed a cupboard filled with gold plate intended only for show and many other instances might be cited to illustrate the widespread profusion at this period.

At the wedding feast of Queen Mary a sideboard of nine stages was exhibited, which was filled with gold cups and silver dishes. Her husband sent to London so large a quantity of plate that it filled ninety-seven chests, loaded on twenty carts.

Queen Elizabeth also followed the example of her father, and surrounded herself with elaborate specimens of the goldsmiths' art. On the occasion of the baptism of James VI. of Scotland, she sent a font of gold to the young prince's mother, Queen Mary, the estimated value of which was one thousand pounds. At a later date she sent a cupboard of plate to James, when Prince Henry was baptized.

During the reigns of Henry VIII., Edward VI., and Elizabeth, the chief portion of the church plate over the country was de-

* Rymer's "Fœdera," vol. xviii. p. 236.

stroyed as "monuments of superstition." In place of "prophane cuppes, bowles, dishes or chalises, hitherto used at masse," the Commissioners cf Queen Elizabeth directed a "fair and comely communion cup of silver, and a cover of silver for the same, which may also serve for the ministration of the communion bread," to be used in every parish in England. The production of these cups, which were mostly made of the same pattern, gave considerable occupation to the silversmiths.

A silver tankard belonging to the Corporation of Norwich, (Fig. 50) is evidently of this date.[6]

Personal ornaments of all kinds were abundantly used at this time by all who could afford them, and the pictures of Queen Elizabeth show her dresses literally covered with jewels. One of the ornaments upon which the goldsmith could exhibit his skill was the pouncet-box,

(*Fig.* 50.) A SILVER-GILT TANKARD AND COVER.
[*Belonging to the Corporation of Norwich.*]

which excited the ire of Hotspur,—

"He was perfumed like a milliner,
And 'twixt his finger and his thumb he held

[6] Peter Paterson was an eminent goldsmith of Elizabeth's reign, and his name is inscribed in one of the cups belonging to the city of Norwich, which were the gift of John Blenerhasset, steward of the city in 1563.

(*Fig.* 49.) QUEEN JANE SEYMOUR'S CUP, DESIGNED BY HANS HOLBEIN.
[*From the drawing preserved in the Bodleian Library.*]

A pouncet-box, which ever and anon
He gave his nose and took't away again."

I. Henry IV. Act i. Scene 3.

The pouncet-box was succeeded in a later age by the elegant
pomander. The annexed illustration (Fig. 51) represents one
of these ornaments of the full size of the original. It was
formed tó hold a variety of essences both fragrant and medicinal,
and each slice contained a specific against infection and ill
odours.

Much of the plate of Elizabeth's time that has come down to
us is now in the possession of various corporations. The colleges

(*Fig.* 51.) A SILVER ENGRAVED POMANDER OR SCENT-BOX.
[*Shown open and closed.*]

of Oxford and Cambridge were endowed by munificent men,
many of whom gave valuable plate as well as money. An
inventory of all the plate given to Winchester College by William of Wykeham is preserved in the muniment-room of the
school.[7] The value of this must have been very great, but none
of it remains now. As these various incorporated bodies increased in importance, the governors gathered around them
handsome specimens of table plate, and we find that in the
sixteenth century the silversmith was very largely employed in
producing cups, hanaps, and tankards.

Richard Fox, Bishop of Exeter, Bath and Wells, Durham

[7] Journal of the Arch. Institute, vol. x. p. 235.

(Fig. 52.) SALT-CELLAR, SILVER-
GILT, XVTH CENTURY.
[Christ's College, Cambridge.]

Presented by Lady Margaret,
Countess of Richmond.

and Winchester in succession, revived the memory of the munificence of prelates such as Wykeham and Waynflete. He founded the College of Corpus Christi, Oxford, and bequeathed to it his crozier, his salt-cellar, his high-standing cups, his silver-gilt low bowl and cover, enriched with a stamped pattern of roses and fleur-de-lis; his rose-water dish, enamelled in the centre; and his two sets of spoons, one with owls and the other with balls or knops at the end of the stem. The crozier and the salt-cellar are said to be among the finest pieces of goldsmiths' work in existence.

The accompanying engraving, (Fig. 52,) represents one of the salt-cellars presented to Christ's College, Cambridge, by its foundress, Lady Margaret, Countess of Richmond. It is of that common form known as the hour-glass salt, and is ornamented with the Tudor rose, the portcullis and the fleur-de-lis. Another gift of the famous mother of Henry VII. to this college is the silver-gilt cup and cover in the form of a Tudor rose, battlemented and engraved with roses and portcullises.

The silver-gilt hanap (Fig. 53), the property of Baron Lionel de Rothschild, is elaborately decorated with moresque ornaments, masks, shells, and heads in relief. Three medallions on the middle of the tazza contain figures of Faith, Hope, and Charity. A figure of Pomona surmounts the cover.

Many of the cups and tankards belonging to the various municipalities and chartered companies of the country date back to the sixteenth century; thus the richly ornamented Grace-cup belonging to the Mercer's Company, which was presented by Sir Thomas Legh, is dated in the last year of the fifteenth century. It is described in the chapter on Enamels.

The silver-gilt cup which was presented to the Goldsmith's Company by Sir Martin Bowes in 1561 (Fig. 54) is dated a few years earlier (1554). The record of the presentation stands as follows :—"June 26th, 1561, Mr. Alderman Bowes freely gave to the Company, in remembrance, a faire gylte standing cup, weighing 80 oz. with a Byrall in the body, in the foote, and in the cover, with a manikin on the cover holding a scutcheon whereon his arms be engraved in an enamel plate of gold."

The very elegant silver-gilt tazza, next represented (Fig. 55),

FROM THE TOP OF
THE COVER.

(*Fig.* 53) TAZZA WITH COVER, SILVER GILT.
[*The property of Baron Lionel de Rothschild.*]

(*Fig.* 54.) SILVER-GILT CUP, ENGLISH, DATED 1554.
[*Presented to the Goldsmiths' Company by Sir Martin Bowes.*]

is the property of Emmanuel College, Cambridge. To the same College belongs another tazza, with the enamelled arms and quarterings of Sir Walter Mildmay, who founded the College in 1584. The upper part of this tazza is decorated with a fringe of nereids and tritons, and supported by four satyrs. Shells and other marine emblems are introduced among the ornaments.

In the next chapter we shall deal with the productions of the seventeenth century. During this period there was even a greater destruction of valuable plate than at the time of the Renaissance. In England many works of art were melted down to obtain money for the belligerents of the Civil war, and later on in France when Louis XIV. had exhausted his treasure by a ruinous and unsuccessful attempt to subjugate Europe he and his subjects were forced to destroy all the plate they possessed.

(*Fig.* 54*a.*) HAND-BELL, SILVER-GILT.
[*Once the property of Mary, Queen of Scots.*]

G

(*Fig.* 55.) TAZZA WITH COVER, SILVER-GILT, XVITH CENTURY (THE GIFT OF THE FOUNDER, SIR WALTER MILDMAY.) [*Emmanuel College, Cambridge.*]

CHAPTER VI.

SEVENTEENTH CENTURY.

FOLLOWING on with our account of some of the chief pieces of collegiate plate we have now to notice the very beautiful tankard of glass and silver belonging to Clare College, Cambridge, and known as the poison cup (Fig. 56), which is only separated in date by a few years from the last specimen noticed in the previous chapter. This cup was presented to Clare Hall by William Butler, a well-known physician in the reign of James I. It obtained its name in allusion to the superstition that on any poison being poured into it the glass would break, and the crystal on the lid become discoloured.

The richly decorated Hanap (Fig. 57) on the accompanying page exhibits the excess of ornamentation which became so prevalent in the seventeenth century. It is said to have been made in the reign of Charles I., and is now the property of her Majesty the Queen.

The next Hanap (Fig. 58), the property of Mr. O. Morgan, is very similar in character, but not quite so highly ornamented.

The cavaliers, as long as they had money to spend, were fond of expending it upon all kinds of gold and silver work, more especially upon jewellery. A puritan named Reeve attacked their extravagancies in his " God's Plea for Nineveh," where he declared that " the wife oftentimes doth wear more gold upon her back than the husband hath in his purse, and hath more

jewels about her neck than their annual revenue doth amount
to."

As the Reformation caused the church plate to be swept into

(*Fig.* 56.) THE POISON CUP, GLASS AND SILVER, XVIITH CENTURY.
[*Clare College, Cambridge.*]

the melting-pot, so the civil war between Charles I. and the
Parliament wrought equal destruction to domestic and corporation plate. Cities and towns were forced to melt their gold and

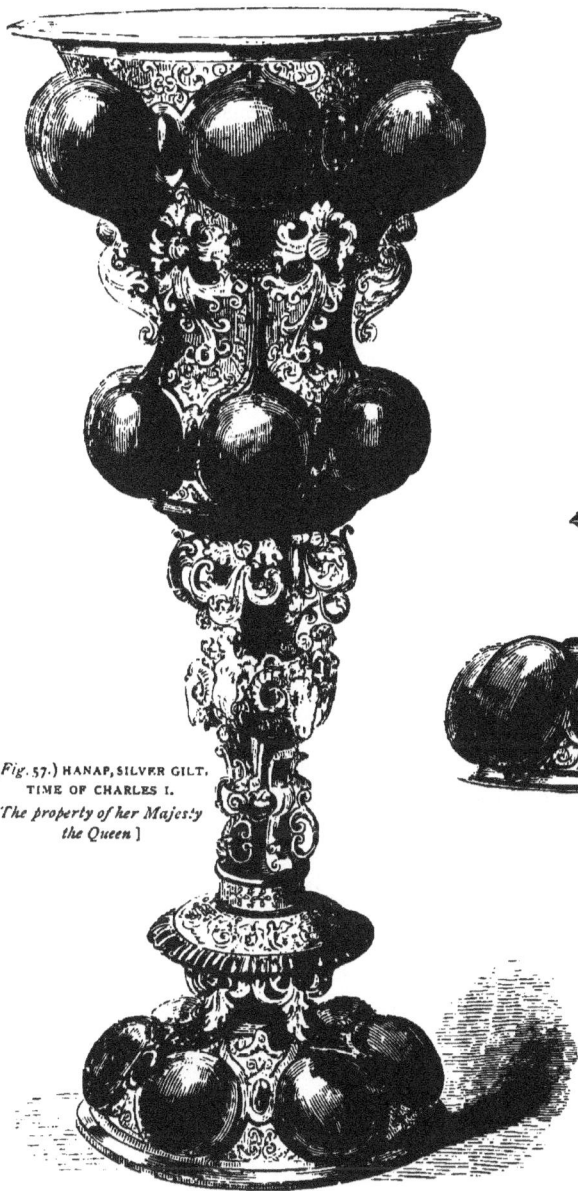

(*Fig.* 57.) HANAP, SILVER GILT, TIME OF CHARLES I.

The property of her Majesty the Queen]

LID OF THE HANAP.

silver for the assistance of one side or other of the combatants, and thus many fine works of art undoubtedly perished.

The cup with cover (Fig. 59) is a good example of the more modern taste introduced after the Restoration. It is silver parcel gilt, ornamented with foliage and birds of perforated appliqué work in frosted silver, detached on a burnished gold ground. This specimen is in the South Kensington Museum.

(*Fig.* 59.) SILVER PARCEL GILT, CHARLES II.
[*South Kensington Museum.*]

St. John's College, Cambridge, possesses an elegant vase and rose-water dish (Fig. 60), which are exceedingly good examples of the beautiful work which was produced by English workmen in the second half of the eighteenth century. The dish bears the following inscription, " Ex dono Edwardi Villiers generosi."

After the Restoration a large number of Maces were made for presentation by Charles II. to those corporations who had aided

(*Fig.* 58.) HANAP, SILVER-GILT, XVIITH CENTURY.
[*The property of Mr. O. Morgan.*]

his father's cause.   Very few of these important articles of the
municipal insignia date further back than this period ; but the
most beautiful specimen that has come down to our time belongs
to the city of Norwich, and was presented to the corporation by
Queen Elizabeth.   It is a chamberlain's mace, and is made of
crystal set in silver—gilt and jewelled (Fig. 61).

Most of the corporation maces are somewhat similar in design,

(*Fig.* 60.) ROSE-WATER DISH AND EWER.
[*From St. John's College, Cambridge.*]

but varieties occur.   The Boston mace of the year 1587 is in the
form of an oar, while that of Dunwich, in Suffolk, is in that of a
bird-bolt, or arrow.

One of the maces of the wards in the City of London was
made in the reign of James I., and seven belong to the reign
of his son and successor.   That of Cheap Ward is dated 1624,
and has the plate mark of that year.   The crown with orb
and cross that now surmount the mace were added in 1678.
The mace of Walbrook Ward was presented in 1634, and that
of Lime-street Ward was made in 1637.

During the seventeenth century there was a general deterioration in the art-workmanship exhibited in the precious metals. The forms of the various objects were generally massive and handsome, but there was an absence of the delicate elegance formerly prevalent. German goldsmiths retained the traditions of their ancestors for the first half of the century, but then by degrees accepted the commonplace ideas of the age. Two of the celebrated Augsburg artists of the earlier period were Matthias Walbaum, who designed the silver images of the famous chest of the dukes of Pomerania, now in the Kunstkammer of Berlin, and Hans Pegolt. Models in lead of the chief works produced by the German gold and silversmiths are kept in the Kunstkammer of Berlin. In the seventeenth century tankards came into general use, and displaced in a measure the lobed cups of earlier usage.

Johann Melchior Dinglinger (1665 —1731) was an artist of great repute. In 1702 he settled at Dresden as goldsmith to Augustus the Strong, elector of Saxony, and adopting the peculiar taste of his time, he produced a large quantity of excellent work in the most grotesque of forms. Many of his productions are preserved in the Green Vaults at Dresden.

The beautiful silver-gilt salver (Fig. 62) in the South Kensington Museum is due to a Flemish artist of the middle of the XVIIth century. The scroll border, which is very gracefully designed, is *repoussé* work. The silver-gilt tankard, enriched with an embossed diamond pattern (Fig. 63), is also of Flemish work.

The next two examples are of Dutch workmanship. Fig. 64 is a silver-gilt tankard of pleasing design, and Fig. 65 is a

(*Fig.* 62.) FLEMISH SALVER (ABOUT 1660).

beaker and cover with ornaments in *repoussé*, and some spirited chasing.

The introduction of tea into Europe caused a considerable development in the work of the silversmith, and silver tea-sets, consisting of caddies, urns, kettles, tea-pots, and cream-jugs, came into general use.

The workers in gold and silver received much encouragement

at the court of France, where luxury reigned supreme. Cardinal Mazarin is said to have possessed fire-dogs and braziers of silver, lustres of crystal and goldsmiths' work, mirrors ornamented with plaques of gold and silver. Louis XIV. was not inclined to be left behindhand in splendour, and he therefore surrounded himself with magnificent objects. Labarte mentions Claude Ballin, Delaunay, Labarre, two of Courtois family,

(*Fig.* 63.) FLEMISH TANKARD, XVIITH CENTURY.

Bassin, Roussel, Vincent, Petit, and Julien Defontaine as among the most skilful artists of their time. Perrault, in his " Hommes Illustres," says that there were by Ballin "tables of such exquisite carving, and so admirably chased, that the material, massive silver though it was, hardly constituted one tenth part of their value; there were cressets, and huge gueridons some eight or nine feet in height, for supporting flambeaux or girandoles; large vases for holding orange-trees, and great barrows for carrying them about; basins, chandeliers, mirrors, all of such splendour, elegance, and good taste in workmanship, that they seemed to give a more correct idea of the grandeur of the prince who had had them made."

Louis XIV. suddenly came to the conclusion that his courtiers were becoming too prodigal, so on the 31st January, 1669, he issued a decree prohibiting absolutely the use of gold plate, and limiting the weight of that of silver, compelling those in pos-

(*Fig.* 64.) DUTCH TANKARD, XVIITH CENTURY.

session of objects in the precious metals to take them to the mint. This was the first attack upon the art of the goldsmith, but later on a worse was to follow. When the treasury was empty by reason of the exhausting wars, and the reverses which clouded the last years of the "grande monarque's" reign, it became necessary to obtain money by some means. The decree of the 3rd December, 1689, consigned to the mint all silver plate used in apartments, such as mirrors, fire-dogs, girandoles, and vases of all kinds. Then it was that nearly the whole of the magnificent secular plate of France was destroyed.

England saw much the same changes as other countries during this period. Very little ecclesiastical plate was produced, and the goldsmiths' art was mainly encouraged by the wealthy nobles for the decoration of their houses. The influence of French art was predominant, and French artists came over to England to

(*Fig.* 65.) BEAKER OF DUTCH WORKMANSHIP, XVIITH CENTURY.

give designs to native workmen. The very remarkable series of silver tables now at Windsor, which were presented to Charles II. by the citizens of London, are described as follows by Sir Digby Wyatt :—

"Exhibiting already in their broken scrolls an anticipation of the impending licence of the age of Louis XIV., they yet display the fine Italian character which the genius of Inigo Jones, and the patronage of the martyr king, the Arundels, Evelyns, and Buckinghams, so warmly fostered during the reign of the two Charleses. Executed almost entirely in thin silver plates of *repoussé* work, planted on in the cases of the large table to a wooden frame, and in the two tripods remarkably well-soldered together, these objects assume the massive grandeur of Venetian work. The drawing and chasing of the acanthus-leaves and running scrolls which constitute the principal ornaments, are in the best style, at once free and delicate ; no trace of the coarseness and prevalent bad drawing of foliage of the antecedent age of Elizabeth, is to be recognized in these details, which are no less free from the heaviness of handling introduced for the most part by the Dutch and Flemish wood-carvers in the reigns of James II. and Anne."[6]

Electrotype reproductions of these tables may be seen in the gallery of the Architectural Court in the South Kensington Museum, where there are also fac-similes of several choice examples of art-work from the regalia in the Tower of London, and many beautiful pieces of old English plate from Knole. In the same gallery are reproductions of several of the finest works in metal,—such as ewers, salvers, and shields now in the Louvre.

Unfortunately the necessities of war were as fatal to the valuable articles of domestic use as they were to the ecclesiastical treasures. The silver toilet services and decorative table-plate in this precious metal, which were so numerous in the royal palaces, were found useful by William III. when he melted them down for the purpose of obtaining the money necessary for his troops.

There is one large branch of the subject to which allusion has not yet been made, as it more properly belongs to the class of a less precious material, we mean military metal-work. When arms and armour ceased to be employed exclusively for personal defence, they rapidly became the vehicle for parade, and the dis-

[6] " Art Treasures of the United Kingdom—Metallic Art," p. 29.

play of a princely taste and magnificence. The most eminent
artists in gold and silver were employed to damascene their
metals upon the steel. The hilts of swords also adapted themselves to the arts of the workers in the precious metals, and
great sums were spent in such ornamentation. When Christian,
the brother of Queen Anne of Denmark, visited England in 1606
he presented James I., among other regal gifts, with a rapier and
hanger, valued at 7000*l.*

(*Fig.* 66.) A SWORD, BELONGING TO HER MAJESTY, AND STIRRUP AND HORSE-BIT.
[*In the Tower of London.*]

CHAPTER VII.

THE EIGHTEENTH AND NINETEENTH CENTURIES.

DURING the reign of Queen Anne great attention was paid to
the art of the silversmith, and much success in design and
execution was obtained. The bold and masterly work of this
period has not been surpassed, and continues to be held in high
estimation.

The eighteenth century was an era of ornamental knicknacks,
and more skill was devoted to the elaboration of snuff-boxes,
chatelaines, and watches than to the more ponderous productions
of a previous period. Although snuff-boxes were common in
the seventeenth century, it was not until the eighteenth century
that their manufacture became in France a special branch of
art. Albert Jacquemart mentions the names of fifteen artists
who were famous as makers of these fashionable appendages.
The snuff-boxes with twisted outline and sharp point are almost
all of the Louis XV. period. Under Louis XVI. the oval form
or rectangular with truncated angles prevailed. The "equipage"
described by Lady Mary Wortley Montagu in her fourth "Town
Eclogue" was an elaborate kind of chatelaine upon which nearly
every conceivable kind of trinket could be attached.

> Behold the equipage by Mathers wrought,
> With fifty guineas (a great penn'orth) bought.
> See on the tooth-pick Mars and Cupid strive,
> And both the struggling figures seem to live.
> Upon the bottom see the Queen's bright face ;
> A myrtle foliage round the thimble-case ;
> Jove, Jove himself does on the scissors shine,
> The metal and the workmanship divine.

Watches when first introduced were clumsy in appearance, but with the improvement of the works a more elegant

(*Fig.* 68.) MARIE ANTOINETTE'S TIMEPIECE.

exterior was obtained, until at one period the beauty of the case was more considered than the trustworthiness of its time-keeping

H

properties. The illustration (Fig. 68) represents a remarkable timepiece which was made for Marie Antoinette.

In the more pretentious works of the goldsmith purity of outline was lost in an exuberance of detail and the rococo style that made architecture ridiculous was carried out to the most extreme extent in gold and silver work. Thomas Germain introduced into his designs leaves of an unnatural vegetation. Claude Ballin's epergnes, with their very complicated and florid ornamentation, had a great success, but the greatest sinner was Just Aurèle Meissonier, who is described by Jacquemart as taking advantage of the talent among the numerous engravers and chasers, and making them put forth their full strength on works with complicated outlines and a superfluity of details. Here the straight line disappeared beneath a mass of senseless ornamentation, where the eye wanders uneasily amid glittering confusion. Other French artists of the eighteenth century who should be mentioned in this place are Rondet, Jacques Roettiers, Jacqmin, Auguste Cheret, and Antoine Bouillier.

(*Fig. 69.*) COVER OF WRITING-TABLE. [*Augsburg work.*]

On the 21st of September, 1786, Louis XVI. issued orders to his plate-keeper to send to the mint "a whole service of plates, dishes, and covers," and when soon afterwards the Treasure of St. Denis was destroyed, the history of the goldsmiths' art in France was wiped out for a time.

But while art was rapidly declining in France, good work was being produced in Germany. The next illustration (Fig. 69) represents the silver-gilt cover of a writing-table of elegant design which was produced by C. Schmidt of Augsburg.

(*Fig.* 71.) SILVER TAZZA, DESIGNED BY MOREL LADEUIL.
(*Repoussé, chased, and damascened.*)

II 2

In England the brothers Adam, architects, adopted in their designs for goldsmiths the classical style which, having travelled from France, became fashionable towards the end of the eighteenth century. A still more eminent artist was Flaxman, who was employed by Rundell and Bridge, the court goldsmiths. His shield of Achilles is well known to students of art.

A century is a sufficiently long period to allow of considerable

(*Fig.* 72.) PUNCH-BOWL, TRAY, AND GOBLETS.
[*By Sassikoff of St. Petersburg.*]

changes in taste taking place during its course. We have seen that the eighteenth century opened with a brilliant display of the silversmiths' art, but later on there was a general decay of good taste, until a revival took place at the close of the eighteenth and beginning of the nineteenth century. Again the art was for a time neglected, to be revived with vigour in our own day.

Modern art is too apt to run into mere imitation, and although

(*Fig. 73.*) SILVER-GILT CASKET.

[*By Cortelazzo of Vicenza.*]

a good copy is always to be preferred to a bad original, no age should be content to produce only copies, however good. The aim of the artist should be by the study of a variety of good designs, so to educate his taste that he may ultimately be able to produce beautiful originals of his own. Each age has stamped its own individuality upon its productions, and no art can stand that does not possess this individuality.

We are able to give here some illustrations of the very fine work that has been produced in the present day.

Mr. Morel Ladeuil has designed some beautiful objects which have been executed by Messrs. Elkington. The Milton shield (Fig. 70) now in the South Kensington Museum, is his most important work. The designs are intended to illustrate the chief incidents of Milton's poems. The circular plaque in the centre represents Adam and Eve in Paradise, on the left are the Hosts of Heaven, and on the right, the Fall of the rebellious Angels. Below, is Saint Michael's victory over Satan. It is *repoussé* work in iron and silver with damascene work (or engraved ornament inlaid with gold wire) introduced.

Another specimen of excellent *repoussé* chasing by Morel Ladeuil is the top of a silver table or tazza (Fig. 71) which was presented by the town of Birmingham to H.R.H. the Princess of Wales on the occasion of her marriage.

Some important statistics connected with the condition of the goldsmiths' and silversmiths' art in France are given in the Report of her Majesty's Commissioners for the Paris Exhibition of 1878.[1] It is there said that "the artists of our day have kept up the glorious traditions of French talent in goldsmiths' work, and placed the trade on a level with other great artistic industries."

About 89,000 kilogrammes (or 196,289 lbs.) of silver are manufactured yearly in the silversmiths' trade, and this represents a value of 17,800,000 fr. (712,000*l.*). This when worked by the silversmith is worth 50,000,000 fr. (2,000,000*l.*) in the following proportions,—

[1] Vol. I. p. 215.

(*Fig. 74.*) DAMASCENED AND CHASED SALVER, BY ZULOAGA OF MADRID.

[*The property of Mr. A. Morrison.*]

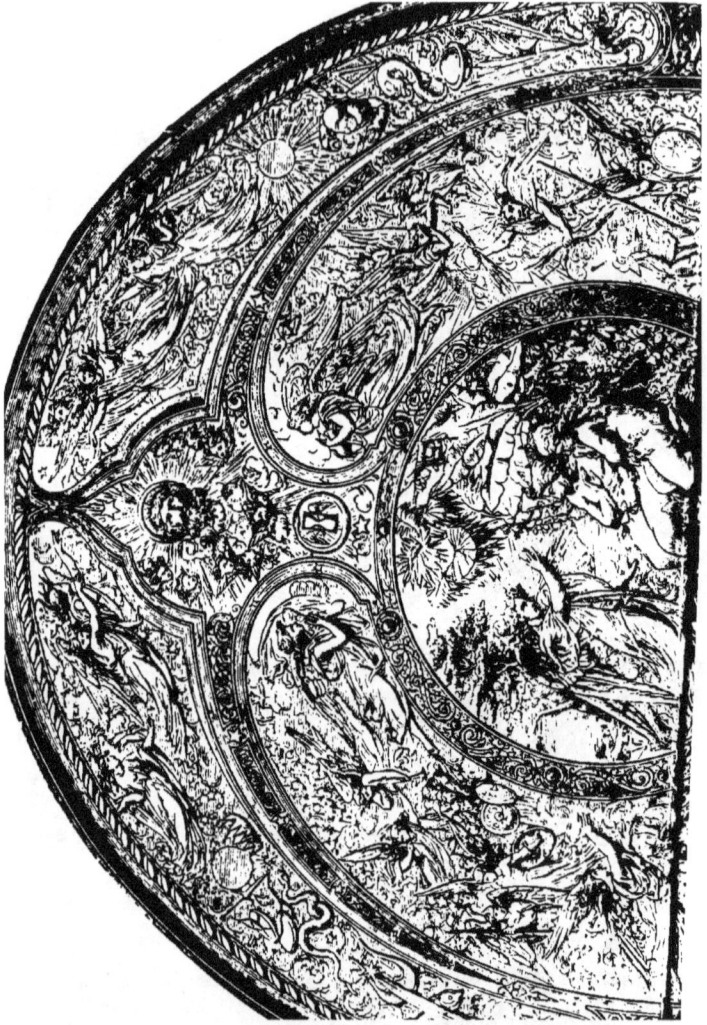

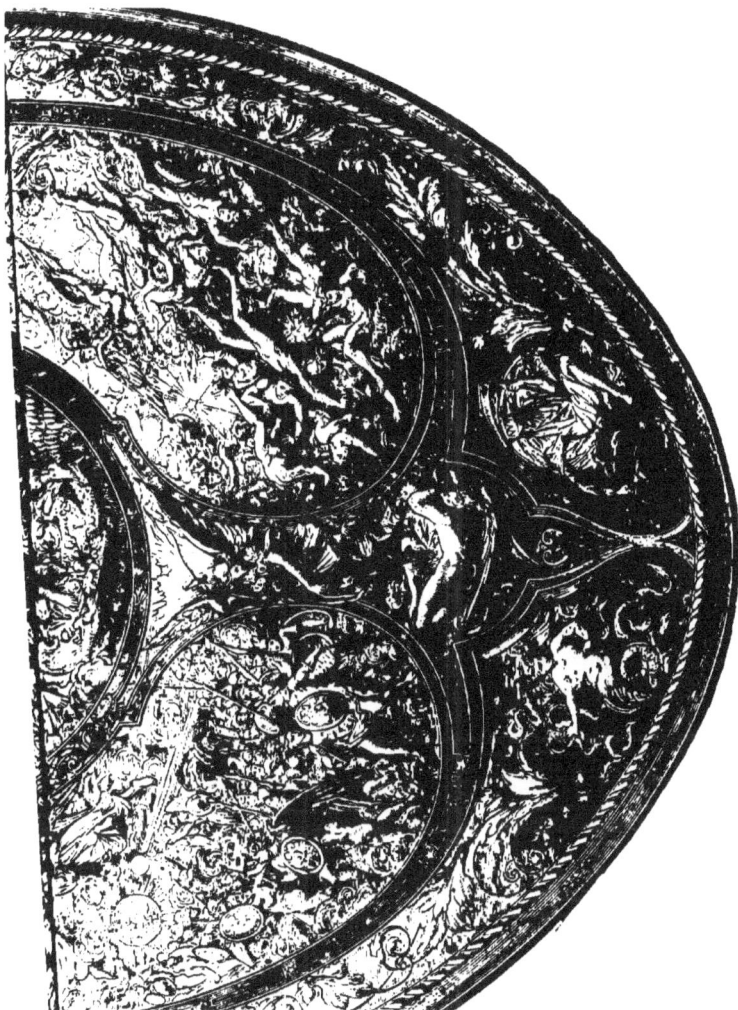

(*Fig. 70.*) THE MILTON SHIELD, BY MOREL LADEUIL, RÉPOUSSÉ AND DAMASCENED.

[*In the South Kensington Museum.*]

Large silver articles	about	18,000,000 fr. (£720,000)
Small „ „	„	5,000,000 fr. (£200,000)
Forks and spoons	„	10,000,000 fr. (£400,000)
German silver and plated articles	„	17,000,000 fr. (£680,000)

The work of the French goldsmith and silversmith divides itself naturally into the two groups of secular and ecclesiastical work.

1. Lay work of all kinds, which comprises artistic pieces, race-course prizes, and competition prizes, embossed work, large statues; gold, silver, and enamelled ornamental furniture; mounted dinner-table "epergnes;" dishes, plate-warmers, candelabra, drinking-cups, enamelled pieces, electro-plate in general, forks and spoons, &c.

2. Church and ecclesiastic goldsmiths' ware, such as sacred vases, chalices, pixes (ciboires), pixes (ostensoirs), cruets for holy oil, &c., necessary for the celebration of the rites of the Church; the episcopal insignia, croziers, crosses, aignières, flat candlesticks, vases for extreme unction oil, croix pectoralis; and for the furniture of the church, such as altars, shrines, candlesticks, crosses, candelabra, &c.

Considerable difference may be noticed in the taste exhibited by the artists of the various countries. Although there is a large amount of cosmopolitanism, the distinctive characteristics of different nationalities are at times very marked.

The examples of Russian silver work shown in the punch-bowl tray and goblets (Fig. 72) are by Sasikoff of St. Petersburg and Moscow.

The elegant and delicately ornamented casket (Fig. 73) by Antonio Cortelazzo of Vicenza belongs to Sir William Drake. It proves that decorative Art of the first kind is still to be found in the country of Cellini.

Zuloaga of Guipuscoa and Madrid is famous for the richness of his designs in a style of art peculiar to himself; the damascened and chased salver here represented (Fig. 74) is a fine specimen of his work; it is between four and five feet long, and the whole surface is engraved most elaborately in the Moresque manner.

CHAPTER VIII.

THE genuine productions of the East have special characteristics of their own, which have remained the same for centuries ; as Albert Jacquemart observes, "the traditions of the past, handed down from generation to generation, form the rules of modern art ; and one is astonished to see reproduced by the most rudimentary means, works of surprising delicacy."

There is one very strong distinction between the productions of Western and those of Eastern art, which consists in this—that the figures of men and animals so much used in Europe are not allowable among Mahometan peoples. With the latter, most designs consist of a skilful combination of geometrical figures with patterns drawn from the vegetable world.

Among the magnificent presents which the Prince of Wales received from the Princes of India, was a fine series of gold and silver plate. These were exhibited at the Paris Exhibition of 1878, and, in common with the other contents of the British Indian Section, were fully described by Dr. Birdwood, C.S.I., in his Handbook to the Section, published in the second volume of the Report of Her Majesty's Commissioners. A prominent object was the silver-gilt service for *pan* and *atar* (betel-leaf and per-fumes), from Mysore, an example of pure Hindu work, in which the shawl-pattern cone of Cashmere manufacture is introduced in the chasing. Some of the ornaments exhibited were, how-ever, bad imitations of English patterns, not originally good, and these contrasted unfavourably with the examples of native art uncontaminated by European influences. The Indian Court contained a large collection of the chased parcel-gilt work of Cashmere. In these the elegant tracery is graven through the gilding to the dead white silver below, by which means a beautiful effect is produced, that is greatly increased by the contrast of colours. Dr. Birdwood, after drawing attention to the origin of Hindu art, which was derived from the contact and mixture of the Aryan immigrants with the local Turanian races, and was subsequently influenced to a great degree by Arabian and Persian art, points to the evident decay of taste among the Indian artists caused by imitation of European designs. The influence of English society, of schools of art and International Exhibitions, upon the progress of Indian art, has been most mischievous.

(*Fig.* 75.) ROSE-WATER BOTTLE, SILVER, INDIAN.
[*In the India Museum, South Kensington.*]

The native has a great genius for imitation, and he naturally thinks that copies of the productions of the ruling race will be more highly appreciated than the older and more national designs of his own people. This evil was very perceptible in a large number of the Prince of Wales' presents; and Dr. Birdwood thinks it fortunate that it was so, because being so conspicuous, this tendency is the more likely to be checked.

The annexed representation of an Indian rose-water bottle in the South Kensington Museum (Fig. 75), exhibits a fine example of beautiful and consistent ornamentation. It is worked in silver, and richly decorated with translucent enamels.

The Indian Court of the Paris Exhibition contained a very remarkable collection of peasant jewelry contributed by Mrs. Rivett Carnac, which consisted of over 6000 objects. The characteristic art of all parts of India was there represented, and Dr. Birdwood has most fully pointed out the chief features of these objects in his admirable Handbook. The silver filigrain work made by the people of Cuttack is the same in character with that of Malta, Denmark, and other countries famous for skill and delicacy in its production. The finest gemmed and enamelled jewelry in India comes from Cashmere and the Punjab, but the Eastern jeweller cares little for the rarity or purity of his gems. His first object is to obtain brilliant combinations of colour, and to unite the stones with the metal setting in a thoroughly effective manner. He does not aim at making the chasing subordinate, but endeavours so to construct his jewel that it may be admired as a whole.

The jewelry of Ceylon, in filigrain, chasing and repoussé, is compared by Dr. Birdwood with the antique jewelry of Etruria. It is remarkable for delicacy of ornamentation and for exquisite finish.

There is a great variety of personal ornaments in India, some of which are used as amulets. There are ornaments for the head which hang over the forehead, earrings and ear-chains, nose-rings and nose-studs, necklaces, strings of precious stones, armlets, bracelets, rings and anklets. Except, as before noticed, where European influence has been brought to bear upon native art, the forms and the ornamentation of Indian jewelry and goldsmith's work generally remain the same as they have been for centuries upon centuries. The native worker in gold and silver obtains a most elaborate surface of ornament, with the smallest possible amount of metal. He lavishes his art in boundless profusion ; so that the intrinsic value of the material is but small in comparison with the value of the product of his consummate skill.   In illustration of this point we may quote an interesting passage from Mons. Burty's " Chefs-d'Œuvre of the Industrial Arts :"—

" We have seen on the neck and arms of a young girl who had been educated in India, necklaces and bracelets of a degree of thinness and suppleness which defied all comparison with our European workmanship.   They were actually as fine and supple as a thread of silk ; and yet not a single one of these threads, in themselves so fine as hardly to be discernible with the naked eye, had given way in the twenty years that she had had them in her possession.   She told us how, that every year, at a certain season, four poor itinerant goldsmiths came and established themselves in a little tent by the roadside opposite her father's house ; they came in, and a few ounces of gold were measured out and handed to them ; then they fixed a small anvil into the ground, squatted on their carpets, and from morning till night they would hammer, chisel, and beat with a surprising degree of patience, ability, and taste.   A handful or two of rice was given them every morning, and about a fortnight afterwards they came and returned the equivalent amount of gold to that which had been lent them, transformed into trinkets and chains so light that Queen Mab might have selected them to harness her butterflies to her chariot.   After which, with stoical indifference they would fold up their tent, remove a few leagues off, and establish themselves at the door of some other nabob."

The Indian section of the South Kensington Museum now contains a magnificent collection of Indian goldsmiths' work, such as has never before been seen.   Dr. Birdwood's Catalogue includes engravings of many of the richest and best jewels, and is a most valuable contribution to the history of the decorative arts in India.

(*Fig.* 76.) RELIQUARY, GOLD, ENAMELLED, EARLY ROMANESQUE.

ENAMEL ON GOLD AND SILVER.

E NAMEL is an easily fusible silicate or glass, to which
colour and the required degree of opacity are imparted by
mixtures of metallic oxides.   It is added to the surface of metals
and pottery in a variety of ways.

There are three distinct classes of enamels as applied to metals,
viz.,—

1. *Inlaid* or *encrusted*, in which the outlines are formed by metal
divisions.

2. *Transparent*, in which the design on the metal is seen
through the vitreous matter over it.

3. *Painted*, in which the outlines are made by a difference of
tint of the enamel itself, completely concealing the metal base.

Of the first class there are two distinct modes of treatment—
the "cloisonné" and the "champlevé."   In the "cloisonné"
process the base is usually a thin plate of gold, and the
enclosures for the enamels are surrounded by a network of gold
filigree bands.   This kind of enamel prevailed chiefly at Con-

stantinople from the eighth to the twelfth century. The other mode of treatment was called " champlevé," because the ground of metal work was cut or dug away to receive the enamels. The metal employed was usually copper. The enamels of Celtic and Roman origin, and the productions of the schools of Germany and Limoges during the twelfth, thirteenth, and fourteenth centuries were thus treated.

The second class, or transparent enamels, were chiefly produced in Italy and France during the fourteenth and fifteenth centuries, and occasionally in the East at a later period.[1] Transparent enamel is usually executed on gold or silver, and the chasing and modelling of the metal is seen through the translucent medium.

The third class includes that mode of enamelling employed at Limoges from the end of the fifteenth to the seventeenth century, and since then in other countries.

It is necessary thus to state the characteristics of the various kinds of enamels ; but in the present chapter we shall only have to refer to the application of enamel to goldsmiths' work.

Mr. Franks has headed a subdivision of his article on " Vitreous Art " with the title " Enamelling among the Ancients ;" but this reminds us of the famous chapter on " Snakes in Iceland," for his object is to show that the art was not known to the ancients. Mons. Labarte has attempted to prove, by collecting a large number of passages from early Greek writers, that enamelling was in existence in their time ; but his theory is mainly founded on the interpretation of the word *electrum* as enamel. Count Ferdinand de Lasteyrie controverted this view, and brought forward evidence to prove that the art of enamelling was unknown to the early classical authors. The later Greeks appear to have had some knowledge of enamelling ; and after the Christian era the Romans cultivated the art. Some enamelled goldsmiths' work was found by Dr. Ferlini, of Bologna, at Meroe, the ancient capital of Ethiopia, about 800 miles to the south of Egypt, which may have belonged to one of the famous queens of Ethiopia. Amongst the ornaments were four golden bracelets ornamented

[1] See Mr. Franks's valuable essay on Vitreous Art in Waring's " Art Treasures of the United Kingdom."

with busts and figures in low relief, and a rich enamelled diaper. Mr. Franks describes the figures as in the Egyptian style, considerably modified by the influence of classical taste, while the patterns of the diaper closely resemble those to be found

(*Fig. 76a.*) BISHOP BERNWARD'S CROSS, ABOUT A D. 1000.
[*In the Magdalene Church, Hildesheim.*]

on works of art of late Roman origin. The colours employed are dark and light blue, white and red, which are kept separate by delicate fillets of metal.

Byzantine enamel was chiefly confined to the ornamentation of the precious metals; and in many instances the enamel was made in small pieces, and applied as a stone would be to the

I

decorated object. Most of the early productions of Byzantine art were destroyed by the iconoclasts.

Bernward's Cross in the Magdalene Church, at Hildesheim (Fig. 76a), is a good representative of the work of the early part of the eleventh century. Bernward, bishop of Hildesheim, tutor to the Emperor Otho III., is said to have executed with his own hands several of the precious objects still preserved in his cathedral.

(*Fig.* 77.) RELIQUARY CROSS, ENAMELLED GOLD.
[*Found near San Lorenzo, Rome.*]

Byzantine influence became very potent in Italy, especially in Venice, and the celebrated *Pala d'Oro,* to which allusion has already been made, is a fine example of the skill of the enamellers of Constantinople. The Right Hon. A. J. B. Beresford-Hope possesses a pectoral cross, or reliquary, of Byzantine cloisonné enamel of the ninth century, consisting of two cruciform plates widening at the extremities, and united together by a silver gilt frame with hinges, forming a box for relics. These early enamels are very rare. The' following is a list of the chief specimens now in existence ; the crown and sword of Charlemagne, of the ninth century, at Vienna ; the Pala d'Oro, of the tenth century, at Venice ; the cup of St. Remi, of the twelfth century, now at Rheims ; the sword of Childeric, at Paris ; the cover of an évangéliaire at Munich ; portions of the Shrine of the Three Kings at Cologne ; the Alfred Jewel (of the ninth century) found near Athelney Abbey in 1696, now in the Ashmolean Museum, Oxford ; and a golden ouche, formerly belonging to Mr. C. Roach Smith discovered in London, and now in the British Museum.[2]

A small cross found at Ringsted, in the tomb of Queen Dagmar, the daughter of Ottocar, king of Bohemia, who died in 1213, is preserved in the museum at Copenhagen.

The enamelled shrine representing the martyrdom and en-

[2] "Catalogue of Antiquities exhibited at Ironmongers' Hall," London, 1861, p. 533.

tombment of St. Thomas of Canterbury (Fig. 76), of Limoges work of the twelfth century, was found in an old mansion, Toddenshaw Hall in Cheshire. The figures, with the heads in relief, are gilt; the background is of blue enamel.

Another shrine in gold and wood, ornamented with enamels, from the Soltykoff collection (Fig. 78), forms a good representation of the early Romanesque art, as exhibited on these objects. Relic crosses were very frequently made of a size that could be conveniently worn. The cross represented in the annexed cut

(*Fig.* 78.) RELIQUARY, EARLY ROMANESQUE. GOLD AND WOOD.
[*Soltykoff Collection.*]

(Fig. 77) was found by Cavaliere di Rossi on the breast of a corpse among the rubbish of the ancient basilica of San Lorenzo, outside the walls of Rome.

The chalice of Kloster Neuberg (Fig. 79) shows both the form and ornamentation which was prevalent in the XIVth century.

Of transparent enamels the famous cup belonging to the corporation of Lynn (Fig. 80) is a good example of the work of the fourteenth century; but Mr. Franks writes that owing to frequent restorations, it is doubtful whether any of the original enamels remain. The cup is of silver, partially gilt, and decorated with figures engaged in hawking, accompanied by symbols of

KNOP FROM TOP
OF COVER.

the chase. It is usually called " King John's Cup,"
but there is no local history to account for this
name. [The knop, or handle of the cover has
been cut off the engraving.]

Some fine examples of the German school of
enamelling are preserved in England. One of
these is the crosier at Goodrich Court, which is
said to have been found in the tomb of Ragenfroi,
Bishop of Chartres, who died about the year 960.
The knop is ornamented with four medallions
formed by the interlacing of stems of foliage, and
the crook is elaborately ornamented.

(*Fig.* 79.) THE CHALICE OF KLOSTER-NEUBERG, XIVTH CENTURY, GOLD ENAMELLED.

· Another is the Warwick bowl (Fig. 81), an enamelled ciborium
in the collection of the Earl of Warwick. The ground of the
subjects was originally blue enamel and the rest of the ground
pale green ; the foliage and the upper and lower borders have
been richly enamelled in bright and strongly-contrasted colours.
The figures are entirely in gilt metal. The subjects represented
are (·1) the sacrifice of Cain and Abel ; (2) the circumcision of

(*Fig.* 80) THE LYNN CUP, SILVER, PARCEL GILT AND ENAMELLED, XIVTH CENTURY.

Isaac; (3) Isaac bearing the wood; (4) sacrifice of Isaac; (5) Jonah issuing from the whale's mouth; (6) the burning bush; and over each subject is a leonine verse describing it. Three of these subjects are the same as those on the famous Bruce bowl.

(*Fig. 81.*) THE WARWICK BOWL.
[*An enamelled Ciborium in the collection of the Earl of Warwick.*]

The Bruce horn (the property of the Marquis of Aylesbury) is a fine specimen of the transparent enamel (Fig. 82), which was much employed by the goldsmiths of Italy, and soon after its introduction into France, became nearly as popular as the native productions of Limoges. This horn bears the arms of the ancient earls of Moray, and probably belonged to Thomas Fitz-

Randolf, nephew of Robert Bruce, and regent of Scotland, who died in the year 1331. The illustration shows the enamelled ornament at the junction of the strap; and on the mounting of the mouth of the horn there is a figure of a king (possibly Robert Bruce), besides other figures.[1]

The peculiarity of the treatment of these transparent enamels consisted in the chiselling of the designs in very low relief. These showed through a transparent coating of enamel of various colours, the outer surface of which was level.

(*Fig.* 82.) PART OF THE BRUCE HORN.
[*An enamelled ornament of the straps with the arms of Randolf, the Earl of Moray.*]

Our next illustration represents a very fine silver and enamel cup (Fig 83), the work of English silversmiths of the fifteenth century. It is now in the South Kensington Museum.

We may here notice the very fine piece of Italian work of the sixteenth century, known as the "Cellini Ewer." The body of the vase is formed of two convex pieces of sard of a rich dark brown colour, carved with radiated convex flutings from the centre. It is encircled by a gold framework round the sides, covered with enamel of white, blue, and green leaves and flowers in pierced work, set with diamonds and rubies; on each side of the sardonyx centre are projecting female heads wearing

[1] An engraving of the horn will be found in "Archæologia," vol. iii. pl. 6.

helmets ending in scrolls ; on the upper half are two enamel figures, that under the spout is a nude recumbent figure, and opposite is the head and body of a man terminating in two dragons' tails ; on the head of this last figure stands a sort of cockatrice or monster with the head, body, and wings of a dragon, and birds' legs, forming a handle which reaches high above the

(*Fig.* 83.) STANDING CUP OF SILVER AND ENAMEL, ENGLISH, XVTH CENTURY.
[*In the South Kensington Museum.*]

mouth of the vase ; between its wings a cupid is seated holding a pair of reins, enamelled with green, yellow, and black, the wings set with rubies and diamonds, and a row of opals on the neck and back. The foot is an oval piece of striated onyx, with a rich border of enamel leaves set with vertical lines of four emeralds and a ruby between each line. This magnificent ewer

(*Fig.* 84.) EWER OF SARDONYX AND ENAMELLED GOLD WORK, ITALIAN, XVTH CENTURY.
Known as the Cellini Ewer. Formerly among the Crown Jewels of France.]

(Fig. 84), which formerly belonged to the French Crown before the great Revolution, is now in the possession of the Right Hon. A. J. B. Beresford-Hope.

The richly ornamented grace cup belonging to the Mercers' Company was presented by Sir Thomas Legh in the last year of the fifteenth century. The maidens' heads and the flagons in the panels are the badges of the company. The foot also rests on three flagons, and has a deep chased border, with a pierced trefoil enrichment. On the cover are the arms of the City of London and the Company, surmounted by a maiden seated with a unicorn reclining in her lap, the word " Desyer " on its side (Fig. 86). Round the cover and cup are bands of blue enamel with letters of silver to this effect,—

" To ellect the master of the Mercerie hither am I
 sent,
And by Sir Thomas Legh for the same entent."

(*Fig.* 85.) PENDANT, ORDER OF ST. GEORGE, XVIITH CENTURY.

Enamels were highly appreciated in England in the sixteenth century ; and Shakespeare has a special reference to them in the *Comedy of Errors*, where he makes Adriana say,—

" I see the jewel best enamelled
 Will lose his beauty ; yet the gold bides still,
 That others touch, and often touching will
 Wear gold."

The poet also twice uses the word in a metaphorical sense as when he speaks of a snake throwing off her enamelled skin, or of water making sweet music as it rushes over enamelled stones.

In the previous pages we have considered, in a somewhat rapid fashion, some of the chief features of the history of the goldsmiths' art. Personal ornaments were amongst the earliest productions in the precious metals, and they will probably continue to be largely called for as long as man remains what he is. Ecclesiastical work, which once exercised nearly all the

TOELLECT

NTENT

(*Fig.* 86.) THE GRACE CUP OF
THE MERCERS' COMPANY,

GOLD AND ENAMEL,
XVITH CENTURY.

energies of the goldsmiths, has now comparatively small influence upon art, at all events in England. The larger and more important pieces of plate are required for corporations, for prizes, and testimonials.

In looking at the splendid examples of ancient art, it is necessary to bear in mind that their production extended over a long period of time. Each school came to perfection, remained stationary, and then was superseded by a new one. The Byzantine gave way to the Gothic, as that in due course gave way to the Renaissance. The main advantage of study is to make us capable of appreciating the spirit of the great designers. We should be induced to emulate their work, and not merely to imitate it, because imitations must naturally be inferior to the originals. There is no real reason why the moderns should be inferior to the ancients in the power of artistic treatment, although it must be confessed that they usually are so.

We have seen how in the earliest times most of the personal ornaments in use were little more than solid lumps of precious metal, and how after a time a proper artistic treatment was introduced. We have seen how the modern Indian follows in the steps of his forefathers, and continues to elaborate his materials with the same fairy-like and elegant design that has prevailed for centuries. All must admit that in the setting of precious stones in England little attempt is made to beautify the gold work, but surely there is no real reason why a true English artist should not emulate the work of Cellini and his school.

What is required is this. The study of beautiful objects should first fill us with admiration for what has been done in past ages, then it should cultivate our eyes so that we are unable to tolerate what is not in good taste, and lastly it should make us capable of elaborating new and living beauty out of the reminiscences of the old.

www.ingramcontent.com/pod-product-compliance
Lightning Source LLC
Chambersburg PA
CBHW021534270326
41930CB00008B/1246